Using Technology for Your Church:
A Guide for Pastors and Church Leaders

By: Jeremy G. Woods

Foreword by: Lorand Soares Szasz

Published by:

FaithVenture Media

Târgu Mureş, România

Jeremy G. Woods

Using Technology for Your Church:
A Guide for Pastors and Church Leaders
Copyright © 2017 by Jeremy G. Woods
Foreword by Lorand Soares Szasz

FaithVenture Media
Târgu Mureş, România
www.faithventuremedia.com

Descrierea CIP a Bibliotecii Naţionale a României
WOODS, JEREMY G.
Using technology for your Church : a guide for pastors and church leaders / by Jeremy G. Woods ; foreword by Lorand Soares Szasz. - Târgu Mureş : FaithVenture Media, 2017
    Conţine bibliografie
    ISBN 978-606-94447-0-2

I. Soares Szasz, Lorand (pref.)

2

All rights reserved. No part of this publication may be reproduced, stored in a retrieval system or transmitted in any form or by any means (printed, written, photocopied, visual electronic, audio, or otherwise) without the prior permission of the author or publisher.

Scripture taken from the *New King James Version*®. Copyright © 1982 by Thomas Nelson. Used by permission. All rights reserved.

Other Works by Jeremy G. Woods

In Peril's Way (2009, 2011) – Eventually will be a mystery series

Fun and Easy Ways to Learn French (2011)

The Missing Ingredient in Our Prayer Life (2012)

Go For It! Motivating Christians to Do God's Will (2013)

Faith Without Borders (2015)

To see more about Jeremy's and his wife's books and updates, visit their website at: www.jeremyandmagdawoods.com

To visit the website for this book, visit www.helpingchurchesgrow.org/churchtechbook

To find out more about FaithVenture Media, visit www.faithventuremedia.com

Dedication

This book is dedicated to God, as I live to serve and please Him. My hope and prayer is that He will use this book to help churches become more effective for Him without compromising their Biblical values.

This book is also dedicated to my wife, Magda. She is a great helpmate for me, and I am very thankful to have her in my life, during all of the life's ups and downs. I look forward to writing more books with her help and encouragement and to encourage her as she also starts writing.

I am very thankful for all the people who have endorsed this book and supported it in any way. For those in our Writing Advocacy Facebook group, I would like to especially thank them as they seek ways to help Magda and me promote our Christian books.

Jeremy G. Woods

CONTENTS

ENDORSEMENTS 9
FOREWORD 13
HOW TO USE THIS BOOK AS A GUIDE 17
INTRODUCTION 23
PART 1: STARTING FROM SCRATCH 27
   CHAPTER 1: WHAT IS TECHNOLOGY? 29
   CHAPTER 2: WHY A CHURCH BOOK ON TECHNOLOGY? 35
PART 2: MARKETING METHODS FOR CHURCHES 39
   CHAPTER 3: A LOGO 41
   CHAPTER 4: GRAPHICS 45
   CHAPTER 5: A CHURCH WEBSITE 47
   CHAPTER 6: SOCIAL MEDIA ACCOUNTS 51
   CHAPTER 7: CHURCH PROMOTIONAL VIDEOS 59
   CHAPTER 8: ONLINE DIRECTORIES 63
PART 3: TECHNOLOGY AS A SPIRITUAL TOOL 67
   CHAPTER 9: NOTE FROM THE PASTOR (BLOGS) 69
   CHAPTER 10: ONLINE SERMON NOTES 73
   CHAPTER 11: RECORDING YOUR SERMONS 75
   CHAPTER 12: CHURCH ONLINE NEWSLETTERS 77
   CHAPTER 13: NETWORKING WITH PASTORS 79
PART 4: FINAL THOUGHTS 81
   CHAPTER 14: DON'T WANT TO DO IT YOURSELF? 83
   CHAPTER 15: YOUR CHURCH TECHNOLOGY PLAN 85
   CHAPTER 16: DANGERS OF TECHNOLOGY 89
APPENDIXES 91
   APPENDIX 1: HOW TO START AN EMAIL ACCOUNT 93
   APPENDIX 2: HOW TO START A WEBSITE WITH WEEBLY 95
   APPENDIX 3: HOW TO START A FACEBOOK ACCOUNT/PROFILE ... 98
   APPENDIX 4: HOW TO START A FACEBOOK PAGE 100
   APPENDIX 5: HOW TO START A FACEBOOK GROUP 104
   APPENDIX 6: HOW TO START A TWITTER ACCOUNT 106
   APPENDIX 7: HOW TO START AN INSTAGRAM ACCOUNT 107
   APPENDIX 8: HOW TO START A PINTEREST ACCOUNT 108
BIBLIOGRAPHY 109
ABOUT THE AUTHOR 111

Jeremy G. Woods

ENDORSEMENTS

"In 'Using Technology for Your Church,' Jeremy G. Woods provides a one-stop-shop for church leaders interested in creating an internet/social media presence. Woods correctly maintains that such technology use can greatly glorify God by drawing more worshippers to Christ. An easy read with a conversational tone, this is a good introduction to the topic."

Cameron D. Armstrong
Missionary, International Mission Board
Bucharest Romania

"Jeremy G. Woods has put together a very clear and easy to read presentation on the church's use of computer technology. His work will be very helpful to those who are new to the web and all of the media sources available. An easy, beneficial how-to read. I recommend this work by a bright young man."

Dr. Eddy Garner
Director of Missions
Colbert-Lauderdale Baptist Association

"'Using Technology for Your Church' should be a mandatory course in online presence for churches and church leaders that haven't yet taken the step towards reaching people through the online medium. It's clear, methodical and thorough. Jeremy G. Woods has created a reliable resource for anyone or any church that wants to develop an online presence.

Through this almost step-by-step guide, Jeremy G. Woods carves the path for leaders to walk outside the church walls and engage with Christians and Non-Christians through social media."

Mircea Țara,
MSc Online Marketing and Award Winning Senior Copywriter at Jazz Communications

"I first became acquainted with Jeremy G. Woods in 2013-2014 as he developed and maintained the website for our Associational four-night, city-wide evangelistic event in Huntsville, Alabama. There were many times, including quite a few late evenings, when I called or emailed Jeremy with updates to our website and I was amazed at how quickly he made the changes. So it doesn't surprise me that he would author a book about technology that would benefit churches and the work of God's kingdom, for the use of technology is his expertise.

From creating a church logo to developing a good church website, which is "the most essential thing for a church in terms of technology," or the use of such social media as Facebook and Instagram, this book explains how such tools can be utilized to convey information and promote church ministry and activities. I particularly like Jeremy's emphasis throughout the book on using technology for the spiritual edification of your church and others. I wish I had this book five years ago when I served as pastor of a local church. I plan to let the eighty-eight churches in my Association know about it."

Dr. Charlie Howell
Executive Director of Missions
Madison Baptist Association
Huntsville, Alabama

"Technology is a powerful tool. If your church or ministry is looking to reach its community, you need to be leveraging technology. This book will help you get started in using technology to reach people inside and outside your church!"

Tim Milner
Lead Pastor
Essential Church

Jeremy has written a very good informative book on how to effectively use technology in the church. This book is filled with great information to help the most novice person involved in communicating with the latest technology of our day. He gives step by step, "how to's" for most everything a person wanting to intersect with the culture today online. What a blessing this book is for the body of Christ!

Dr. Larry Inman
Senior Pastor, All Nations Church
Huntsville, Alabama

"In this book, Jeremy G. Woods correctly emphasizes the importance of using technology as a way for churches to reach more people. Not only does he make a convincing case of its importance, but he proceeds to simply explain how this can be done. A must have for churches that currently have no website or a very limited one.

Todd Panter
President
Church Strengtheners

In our current culture, it is simply a matter of good stewardship to utilize technology for the advancement of the Gospel. Jeremy does a great job of providing very practical information to help even the most "technically challenged" person with the confusing and often complicated world of technology. This resource provides step-by-step instructions and covers a wide variety of relevant topics for pastors and church leaders who realize the potential impact technology can have for the Kingdom."

Kevin Madden
Senior Pastor
First Baptist Church, Washington, GA

In order to share the Gospel and minister to the world around us, we have to speak the language of the people. In many cases today, that happens to be the language of technology. Jeremy G. Woods has produced a useful introduction to some of the most relevant tools available, helping pastors and church leaders minister to people near and far. I highly recommend this book.

Mark Milas
Executive Pastor, Bridge Church
Dallas, TX

FOREWORD
By Lorand Soares Szasz

"I tell you that if these should keep silent, the stones would immediately cry out" (Luke 19:40).

Every time when I feel that I am not using my abilities to the maximum to bring the message of salvation further, I remember this verse in the Gospel of Luke.

The first time I read this passage, technology like today's technology didn't exist. Smartphones, tablets, projectors, social networks, YouTube, or other similar means of communication didn't exist. The stones crying out was more of a metaphor in my mind.

But, in the last few years, things changed radically. From self-driving cars to text message advertisements sent at the time you pass in front of a store, I have seen many things! Technology has developed so much that we can promote our product or service in a creative, efficient, and rapid way.

We see presidential elections won with the help of social networks, we see dictatorships fall because of a revolutionary movement started on Twitter, we see the refining of promotional messages to the smallest details based on the psycho-ethno-demo-sociographical profile. We see how marketing experts succeed to "package" a message so well that the decision to buy a product or service becomes purely emotional.

All these methods and ways of promoting can be used in a positive or negative sense. Just as television in its age of glory was used to destroy spiritual values, at the same time, it was used to transmit Jesus' gospel.

It's a great loss that all these tools and ways remain unused by the church. It's a shame that we don't "promote our own product," that is, Jesus and His message, by using the most modern and efficient methods.

If in the past few years, the concern of a pastor or a preacher was that the congregation would not fall asleep in church, things are completely different nowadays.

Video games, social networks, television, and video-sharing sites have captured our attention. The pastor competes with YouTube, not with people falling asleep. A church member prefers to stay in the comfort of the home and watch a sermon on YouTube or something else that may even distract him from God.

All of these force everyone who is involved in the leadership of a church to raise the standards. "Competition" forces us to promote ourselves more efficiently, to be present in the social environments, and to share the message of Jesus through those same methods that are used in any successful company.

We have the most important product "to sell." We have the most valuable "service to give." We have the responsibility to make His message get to the end of the earth. We must train ourselves and use the most efficient methods in this sense.

Jeremy has succeeded to build an efficient guide for this purpose. In the lines of this book, you will discover simple steps on how you can have an online presence for your church and, if you already have it, how you can use it more efficiently.

It's time that we "talk"; if not, stones will do so instead of us!

Lorand Soares Szasz *is an entrepreneur and one of the most sought experts in accelerated growth of businesses. He helps tens of thousands of companies to promote their products and services more efficiently. Being raised in a Christian family and closely observing his father's activity, who is a pastor, Lorand has on his heart the holy work of sharing the message of Christ in the most efficient way.*

Jeremy G. Woods

How to Use This Book as a Guide

This book is not meant to be a book you read and then simply forget but to be put in practice by pastors and church leaders for their churches. Therefore, it is highly suggested that you read this book as a tutorial to get your church using the various methods to not only promote your church but also to grow your church Spiritually. Also included is a template on how to create a Church Technology Plan (and a free download of the template is available on my wife's and my website, at the link listed later in this book). Please feel free to download and print the template so you can use it.

It's easy to look at the topics of technology and marketing as secular topics, but when they mean the ability to change lives for Christ beyond the reach of your church's walls (and even beyond your own community), technology becomes a way for your church to do outreach, and marketing your church to your community is a way to bring people to your church. Marketing your church through technology does not mean that you should stop doing the methods you already do (if they are Biblically sound), because ultimately human interaction is what we were created for, and using technology is only one way of promoting your church.

If no one finds his or her way into your church through the methods described in this book, but you do have people "virtually" discover your church online and their lives change, your having read and applied this book's methods will be worth it. After all, you're in the ministry to build your own church up, but you're also in ministry to reach people with the Gospel of Christ. This is the ultimate goal of the church, to see people from all nations and people groups worship God.

There are different types of multimedia that are useful for churches and their pastors and leaders. Some types are very useful for free or cheap promotion of the church, while others are useful for networking and for Spiritual growth.

A church needs a good logo for consistency in

church promotion. See Chapter 3 for more information about logos.

You see graphics all over the internet, and it's a great way to promote your church. See Chapter 4 to see how you can create graphics for free.

A good website is the most essential thing for a church in terms of technology. Just sticking essential information on a website is not enough. It needs to look fairly professional (even if it is not done by a professional). There is more information about how to do this in Chapter 5, the chapter on websites.

Facebook, Twitter, Pinterest, and Instagram are four social media sites that are not only free but very useful for churches. Facebook and Twitter are the most essential of these four, but Pinterest and Instagram are good for posting pictures created using easy and free tools. These social media sites are covered in Chapter 6.

Did you know that you can create a video for free for your church? And it really doesn't take very much time to figure out how to create. Learn more in

Chapter 7 about how to create these videos yourself – and save your church a lot of money (though if your church has a budget, a professional one is better).

Your church is probably already listed on at least one online directory (and can be listed on much more for free). Check out Chapter 8 to learn about how to edit your church's page on YellowPages.com.

Do you have something to say to your congregation every week, beyond your weekly sermons? You can put it online and tell your congregation how to access it by creating a blog. Find out how to create a free blog in Chapter 9 (and find out how to put it on your church's website.

There is a phone and tablet app called Bible+ (or YouVersion) that allows churches to broadcast notes for the congregation during the service so that everyone follows along with the outline (and others not in the church can also view this outline so that you have an outreach directly from your church). Read more about this in Chapter 10.

When I preach, I place a device that just about

everyone has and then upload it on the internet for free. Curious about how to utilize this free way to record your sermons (and even more free and paid ways)? Chapter 11 has the answer.

Does your church have a church bulletin or church newsletter? You can allow the bulletin to be put on the internet (publicly or privately) where members can see and share the information more easily (and church members who are living elsewhere or homebound can keep up with the church). Want to know more? Find out in Chapter 12.

Does your denominational association have a weekly or monthly meeting where they get encouragement and ideas from other pastors in the area? Imagine being able to get encouragement and ideas from pastors around the world whenever you want. Find out how in Chapter 13.

The last part of this book deals with delegating the job of communications and technology if you realize that this is not something you want to do yourself. There is a technology plan template for your church included in the book as an example (as well as a link to download the PDF version of the plan from my wife's and my website). Also, there is a warning about the use of technology, as there are some risks in using it. Also, included toward the back of the book are some appendixes to facilitate creating social media accounts for your church (including Appendix 1, which shows you how to create an email account, if you don't already have one, since you'll have to have an email account for pretty much any social media account you create).

I will also mention that I recently have created the website www.helpingchurchesgrow.org to be a resource for pastors and church leaders, including a blog that I plan to update with new ideas on how to grow your church. Be sure to check it out, as I plan to add more on a monthly basis. Also, if you want to write an article for it, you can send me an email on the contact page so that I can put guest blogs on there as well.

Introduction

This book is written with the assumption that you are a pastor or church leader. Also, it is written with the assumption that your church has not hired a full-time multimedia staff member and that you have to do all the multimedia promotion for your church yourself.

Therefore, this book starts at a basic level of understanding, but it does not attempt to teach the reader how to turn on and operate a computer. There are many books and classes for that; this book's focus is church promotion from a technological standpoint.

If you fit the description of an ideal reader, I urge that you continue reading this book to gain more understanding of how to promote your church to reach the next generation (but to do so without falling into the sin of making your church too worldly to attract the world).

Starting from the basics of what technology and multimedia are, I will attempt to bring you from not understanding about social media to being able to readily promote your church without breaking your church's budget (and even how to take advantage of completely free ways of doing so). With the purchase of this book, you have opened the world of technology to your church without even having to spend another dime (other than a computer or internet access if you do not already have them). This book does, however, include paid options as well. Next, I will also show you ways to use technology to build up your church (and others) spiritually.

Too many churches close their doors because their church has had too few members remaining, and their congregation's remaining members either died off or got too sick to come to church because they were homebound. This book intends to open your church more to a multi-generational level. Also, too many churches split because of a desire from some of the church members to have contemporary services and some of the church members wanting the hymns in services only. This book is not meant to address these further problems; however, I do want to encourage you to stay true to God's Word when facing issues that may cause the church to become too worldly in its methods to reach the younger generations.

An important point to keep in mind is that you need to keep the main thing the main thing. The reason your church exists is to glorify God and to get others Spiritually fed, so if you get great at using technology but lose the focus of your church, you have lost sight of the goal of the church and have brought people away from serving God.

Part 1: Starting from Scratch

Chapter 1: What Is Technology?

Chapter 2: Why a Church Book on Technology?

Chapter 1: What Is Technology?

According to the Merriam-Webster dictionary's definition, technology is "the practical application of knowledge especially in a particular area" (Merriam-Webster's Dictionary). Multimedia is an application of technology. Here is a definition of it: "a technique (as the combining of sound, video, and text) for expressing ideas (as in communication, entertainment, or art) in which several media are employed" (Merriam-Webster's Dictionary).

Within the last century, today's technology has not only come into existence but has also become prevalent in many people's lives. It is how they buy groceries, it is how they communicate with people (especially long-distance), and it is even how they choose a church. "It might not be surprising that young adults are more likely to look online for information about a congregation, given that younger Americans, in general, are more likely to use the internet than older adults" (Masci 2016). Myself included, I tend to look for a church online rather than going somewhere in person to see how it is. This means that there is a major shift from the 1800's of people going within a specific distance from their house (since cars weren't even invented until the end of the 19th century!) to now people travelling hundreds of miles (even sometimes for work) and having contact with people all over the world through technology. With this change in how technology is used in daily lives, it is still the responsibility of the church to fulfill the Great Commission found in Matthew 28. A part of fulfilling this Great Commission should be done through properly getting people informed about the church through ways that they normally find out about other things. In this manner, it is not worldly to promote the church through the same ways they learn about local events or what's on television; instead, it's using the resources that God has given us for the furtherance of His Kingdom.

If we are going to reach the next generation, who will be the future leaders of the church, then we should attempt to reach them in Biblically-appropriate ways. In the South of the United States, where I am from, there is a church just about on every corner. This means that getting people to know about your church is going to take effort on the church's part, especially if you want your church to grow in number. More importantly than growth in number, of course, is Spiritual growth, which is another responsibility that the church should focus on; however, the church's growth in members is a very important aspect of the church as well.

Worldly methods that bring in crowds are not Biblically sound. "I beseech you therefore, brethren, by the mercies of God, that you present your bodies a living sacrifice, holy, acceptable to God, which is your reasonable service. And do not be conformed to this world, but be transformed by the renewing of your mind, that you may prove what is that good and acceptable and perfect will of God" (Romans 12:1-2, NKJV). When talking about using technology, however, this is a different strategy than bringing in loud music or lights and smoke that attract the younger generation.

When I refer to using technology for your church, I am referring to promoting your church to your community through social media, a web presence (so others can find out more about your church), putting sermons online (so that others can be fed the Word of God), and using technology during the service that allows everyone to see song lyrics during worship or be able to read the Bible from the screen. Putting the Bible verses on the screen does not mean that they should not follow along with their Bible, but it allows those who are not familiar with the Bible to still be able to read.

I am generally very wary of books or articles that talk about church growth (even though marketing was my college major) because they seem to lead into how the church needs to bring worldly methods into the church. Not all church growth books talk about worldly methods to bring into the church, obviously, but that's the general characterization of church growth books. However, I am not convinced that using technology to "promote" the church should be considered a worldly method. This is a way that those in my generation and younger will be more likely to find out about your church.

Technology can bring the world closer together, in a way that has not happened before. Now people who are in the middle of a move, for instance, can find out about things in the city where they're moving to in an easier manner. Whenever I move to a new city, I tend to check out the churches in the area online before I move and generally decide ahead of time which ones I plan to visit. By searching the city on social media, people can find out information about churches that they cannot usually do by anything other than a visit (even hear or see church sermons online). However, if the church does not have a presence on social media and the internet, people searching for a church may not find a church that is not online in some manner, especially if the church is not centrally located in the city or town.

Chapter 2: Why a Church Book on Technology?

Isn't every church on the internet, on Facebook, etc.? No, this actually isn't the case. There are many churches still without an internet presence (or with a website that looks like it was made about 20 years ago when websites had a different look). This statement is not meant to offend anyone; it is just true that churches should not only have a website but also have a good website.

It is the church's goal to see everyone worshipping God. With this goal in mind, isn't it important for people to be aware of your church? This is what marketing does. Whether or not we like to use the term "marketing" for churches, we can probably agree that it is important to get people into the church, and marketing creates awareness of the church.

There are many types of multimedia available for your church's use. Today's technology is easily and readily usable by just about anyone. Social media is one of the most popular forms of communication now, and it is one of the quickest and best ways to get out your church's information. Technology also allows for people to grow Spiritually, through reading pastors' blogs and watching sermons on the internet. Also, through social media such as Facebook and Twitter, conversations happen where people grow Spiritually through sharing ideas and exchanging commentary on Biblical passages.

The appearance of the internet has given companies and churches an inexpensive and easy platform to promote themselves, and this is now where people tend to find out information. Obviously, word of mouth still plays a very significant role in getting someone to come to church and for helping them become a Christian, but social media is another big factor to people having awareness about a church.

A website plays a very important role in being the main source of information about the church. Anything that the church posts on the internet or hands out to the church or the community should at least have the church internet address placed on it. Near the end of the book, you will find appendixes to help you create accounts that your church can use, everything from email to websites to social media accounts. You can refer to these as you begin to build your church's internet presence.

Jeremy G. Woods

Part 2: Marketing Methods for Churches

Chapter 3: A Logo

Chapter 4: Graphics

Chapter 5: A Church Website

Chapter 6: Social Media Accounts

Chapter 7: Church Promotional Videos

Chapter 8: Online Directories

Chapter 3: A Logo

As you'll learn later, the most important technological aspect a church should have for its congregation is a website. However, a website cannot effectively be done without having a good logo for the church. A logo adds uniformity in promotion and in marketing, and it also enables something in marketing called "branding." While I don't intend to equate church marketing to secular marketing, therefore I don't want to refer to creating a logo for your church as branding your church, I also do want to inform you of a few terms throughout this book so that you understand better the marketing world.

Having a logo means that, no matter what you use to promote your church, it is recognizable that it came from the same person or organization. Having a logo does not equate to branding, but it is a start to creating uniformity. An important thing to note is that, when you create a logo for your church, you don't have to use it everywhere (for instance, on your church bulletins). I would suggest, however, that you do use your logo on your electronic newsletters (talked more about in a later chapter).

To start with, it's important to recognize what a logo is and what it isn't. A logo involves an image, usually along with text (think of all the products that you know, and you have an idea of what a logo is). "A logo identifies a company or product via the use of a mark, flag, symbol or signature. A logo does not sell the company directly nor rarely does it describe a business" (Just Creative 2010). Of all the products that you know, especially ones without words but a picture, can you recall what product it is just by seeing the logo? That is how helpful a logo is to building a brand. This is not exactly what your purpose is when using a logo for your church, but it does help when realizing what a logo does when it is put on a product. While a church is not a product (or even a brand), logos do come in handy to develop consistency in promoting the church through the internet and social media. A logo can be put on a web page, a newsletter, social media sites, etc. Typically speaking, a logo isn't text using a certain font and colors, while in my opinion, that can also be a logo. A simple logo, but still a logo. There are ways to create these, but there are also ways to create logos with pictures. Be sure to post the logo on social media, on your website, and on other print materials to make the message uniform that you are sending.

Doing a simple search on a search engine, websites that allow you to design free logos are hard to find. When it says they are free, usually it means that you get a low-quality graphic, which isn't beneficial for your church. Other times, you'll run into sites that promise something for free, but really what is free is designing the logo. Then, once you've designed the perfect logo, they say you have to pay to download it.

There are some good options available that are inexpensive. One good site is www.fiverr.com, which allows for designs for many types of multimedia or text. Sellers put what they do or create online and tell you what price. It used to be $5 for products as a base price, but now people can list their services for more as a base price.

The most I would suggest you pay for a logo is $50, but be sure that you can get an editable file along with the logo, if possible. Even if you may not be as knowledgeable yourself on how to edit it, maybe there's someone at your church who can edit files or someone in your community or network.

Canva.com does have a very good free logo designer. If you visit www.canva.com/create/logo, you can test different logo design possibilities. It is free, though many picture options are available for $1. You will need to create an account at Canva (which is free) to be able to design the logo. Once you are done, you can download the logo and use it. Another free one is onlinelogomaker.com. Once you register with a free account, you can get started with making your free logo (and it also is a simple logo to make). While I'm sure more exist, it's hard to find ones that are completely free.

Chapter 4: Graphics

To share information easily and in an interesting format, you will need to learn how to make graphics. Graphics are a great way to create interest in your church, and they provide a way to convey information at the same time. Do you need to promote your Christmas Eve service or your Resurrection Sunday service? A graphic will be able to give people the information they need, and you can also list your church's website at the same time.

A great site to visit to create free graphics is pablo.buffer.com. They have photos already on the site, but you can also upload your own. You can add different types of text, and you can end up with a good graphic to post on your website, Facebook, Twitter, Instagram, and Pinterest. They even allow you to create one that best fits these social media websites. Once you log in, you can view images or even search by name for a topic (they have photos of churches, even photos that would go well for your Resurrection Sunday event). Once done, you just click "Share and

Download." I would suggest you download it and then upload it on your website and on social media sites. Canva.com (mentioned in the logo chapter) also lets you create free graphics. There are more good websites out there. You can take the time to research the one that you enjoy using the most.

If you need to make sure that it looks like a good graphic, you can check with a church member or community member before you post it. It's a good idea to have someone check major graphics and social media posts anyways before you post it publicly. Of course, you'll be able to delete it from the site if you need (though it doesn't permanently remove it from the internet altogether), but it's still a good idea to have a system in place to make sure that everything is accurate and looks good before you officially make the post.

Chapter 5: A Church Website

One of the most important tools that a church should have to promote itself (and to help its members to grow spiritually) is a good church website. Any other form of multimedia, in my opinion, is a bonus to the promotion of a church. If you have used the internet at all, you have been to a website. Having a church website is like the church's business card, in a sense. It is a place you can tell others about in order to find out about your church. You can have as much as you want on a church's website, but it shouldn't be too complicated for users, either. Here are the main basics you will want:

- Welcome page
- About Us page
- Our Staff page (with bios, photos, and emails)
- Ministries page (or even a page for each ministry)
- And a Contact Us page (including email address and church address)

Another thing you need to add somewhere on the

website to find easily is the times of the services during the week (and what each service is). Also, make sure to have a picture of your church, preferably on the Welcome page of the website so that visitors will know what to look for when looking for your church.

You will want to make sure to update the web page regularly (and you can even have a page to list church events or to show the church's calendar). A bonus is to add a member's only section where church members can see things that are not open to the public (such as a church directory). This is not required, but it is a way that your members can see things that you don't want everyone to be able to see.

A church website can be free, but most likely, you cannot get a website for free that has its own domain name (unless someone donates the domain name for the church). A domain name is what you type in with the www part of the website name. A domain name ends with .com, .org, .net, or many other endings (recently a lot more of these domain name extensions were added to be selected). A .com or a .org would be preferable for a church, although .church is now also a possibility. I would personally suggest sticking with .com or .org just to make it easier for people to remember; however, other people may have different opinions about the new domain name extensions.

You will need to choose a website that helps you design your website. You can pay someone to create it for you or you can design it yourself. There are 'drag-and-drop' methods (like Weebly.com) that allow you to create a website very easily. There are paid accounts for website builders like Weebly.com, but sometimes a free account helps you accomplish what you need to be accomplished. Drag-and-drop methods are very good since you won't have to learn HTML (the programming language for websites) in order to have a professional-looking website. Instead, they rely on templates, which give you a website that stands out and need no programming for you to use. You can see how to start a Weebly account in Appendix 2.

A very important thing to keep in mind is that the website needs to look presentable. "Your church website is your first impression. It needs to represent who you are as a church. Think of it like the upkeep of your building. You wouldn't let your facilities fall apart, so why would you let your website look bad?" (Clark 2012). Sometimes people will base their decision on whether or not to visit a church based off of the church's website. While this is not a good spiritual decision, it's because, as Clark said, "Your church website is your first impression." This is a new aspect of Christianity that didn't exist 100 years ago, but we cannot ignore the fact now that a website is important for a church, and it is very important now that your sermons can be put on there as well.

Chapter 6: Social Media Accounts

This chapter will attempt to cover what you need to know about Social Media such as Facebook, Twitter, Instagram, and Pinterest to promote your church. Look at the appendixes at the back of the book to see how to start the social media accounts.

Facebook

Facebook has been available to the public, ages 13 and above, since 2006, and it doesn't seem like it will ever stop being used by people. It has many advantages, as it has many users worldwide. Being the most popular social media site, it is sure to be the best social media site to use to promote your church. You can use Facebook for personal use if you don't already, but in this book, we will mainly look at methods for Facebook pages and Facebook groups (two different things with two separate audiences). In order to create either, though, you will need your own personal **Facebook account** (and according to Facebook terms, it needs to be your own personal Facebook account that you create, not one for your church).

A **Facebook page** is a public way of letting people know about your organization (in this case, your church). People "like" a page to get updates about it (although sometimes people unfollow a page because they get too many updates but still "like" it on Facebook to show public support). This means that not everyone who "likes" your page on Facebook necessarily sees your post (and then you factor in Facebook post algorithms — a process that Facebook uses to sort the posts that they think you should see and weed out posts that they think you won't like or won't want to see).

While people can create "visitor posts," people other than those who have the authority to write on the account cannot make a post that is easily seen by others (unless someone goes to the "visitor posts" section on the page). However, with Facebook groups, other people can post. A Facebook page is a one-way street for conversations (though people can comment on posts). You should regularly post on your church's Facebook page, as it is a free way to promote your church.

A **Facebook group** allows you or other church members to post things useful for your church's members (but not necessarily useful or appropriate to share publicly for everyone to see). You don't have to create a Facebook group if you have a Facebook page for your church but, if you ever want to post things that are not public, you should consider creating a Facebook group and using it within your church.

You don't have to just post photos and videos in the Facebook group. You (and others) can also post files or create a poll or even post a live video (including one of your church service). You can encourage members to post prayer requests and encourage members to check the group for updates and for prayer requests from you and other members. Sunday School classes also can have their own Facebook group to share things within their own class on Facebook (prayer requests, announcements, encouragement, Bible verses, etc.). You can see how to start a Facebook account, page, and group in Appendixes 3-5.

Facebook ads are another way of promoting through social media. They can be created in a matter of minutes. Ads Manager can be found under the Explore tab to the left of Facebook. You can promote a post or photo (e.g. a graphic that you create and post) to a specific demographic. Facebook allows you to choose the location, interests, gender, and even age of the people you want your ad to target. Within a couple of hours, the ad is generally approved or declined. For starters, you could set it at the minimum amount of money to be spent in order to test out its effectiveness. They even provide hints on how to make an effective ad. You can select how long the ad will run.

<u>Twitter</u>

Twitter is unique when it comes to social media sites. It has one main purpose: to send out short quotes or updates. However, when promoting a business (and therefore also a church), it is a great tool to use. On Facebook, most people don't necessarily add people that they don't know to be "friends" on Facebook, but on Twitter, people "follow" many other people. While some of these followers may not be "real" followers, it is a great way to get potential church members. You can search for certain keywords for people's profiles, and you can also use the "hashtag" feature (#) to find people with similar interests (for example, the city where your church is located, someone interested in missions, etc.).

The best part is that it is free to have an account. You can also do paid advertising on Twitter, but I would highly suggest to just follow people and get people following your church on Twitter as a start. Be sure to post regularly. It can be encouraging quotes, a promotion of Sunday's sermon, or whatever you want to put...in 140 characters or less. Of course, you can do a continuation of the last post, if you want. It can be challenging to say what you need to say in 140 characters or less, but fortunately you can add graphics in the post and also give a link to a website.

This does count towards the 140 characters, but it also allows you to get your point across easier; for example, your Twitter post could be a short summary of a blog that you posted, and then you put a link to the blog post within your Twitter post.

Another way to use Twitter is to post videos (especially Sunday's sermon). Your ministry should extend beyond your church if you do want to reach souls, and through posting your videos, you will possibly see more souls saved. One thing about Twitter is that many posts go on Twitter each minute so not all of your posts will be seen by many people. Therefore, you shouldn't base your entire social media ministry on using Twitter, but it is a great tool. You can see how to start a Twitter account in Appendix 6.

Instagram

Instagram is used for photos, and it can be used to promote church-wide activities. You should already do photos for Facebook and Twitter that mention quotes that are beneficial or that promote church activities, so an extra step would be creating an Instagram account and posting them there. Use the information from Chapter 4 on Graphics to be able to create the graphics that you would post on Instagram. Be sure to put on your church's website a link to your church's Instagram account. In order to post on Instagram, you'll need to use a smartphone that has access to the Instagram app.

You can follow church members, and other people as well. Be sure to post graphics that you create, as well as post photos from special events. Instagram is a great advertising tool that is free, so be sure to take advantage of the fact that you can have a free account and use it. You can see how to start an Instagram account in Appendix 7.

Pinterest

Pinterest is a social media tool that enables users to share things that interest them. Many types of things can be put on Pinterest. I use it to collect a list of locations for filmmakers to "scout" for their movies, as well as to promote my books and to create interesting images with Christian quotes.

Your church can put up Pinterest "pins" to promote the events that your church has. Also, if you design graphics throughout the year, you can post those on Pinterest as well. If any church members have a Pinterest account, you can follow them so that they can share your church's pins on their Pinterest account as well.

You don't need to just create your own graphics to pin on Pinterest. If you find a Christian pin that is encouraging, you can repin someone else's pin that they posted. Using Pinterest as part of your church can become part of your Christian ministry because you are encouraging your members and others. You can see how to start a Pinterest account in Appendix 8.

Chapter 7: Church Promotional Videos

Have you seen sermon series videos during a church service or seen a promotional video done for a church and wondered how your church could ever afford something like that? You can actually do something like it yourself, and for very little money involved. You could do it for free, but I'd suggest one purchase (that is $100 per year) that will make it even better.

I will assume that you are using Windows (I don't know much about Mac computers, but I have used them before, and they do have similar programs available). Your computer probably came with a program called Windows Movie Maker. If not, you should be able to find a free legal download online. Once you have installed it, open it and insert a photo or video that you want to add to the video.

If you need free legal video clips, there is a site I use called www.pixabay.com. You can search for the photo or video that you want (you can change the box that says "All photos" to say "Videos" in order to search for videos). They have a lot of photos and videos, and you can get them from the website for free, even for commercial use, without having to give them attribution. Most sites seem to require that you pay a one-time or monthly fee, but this website does not require a fee.

The website www.audioblocks.com does cost $99 per year for downloads of music, sound effects, and loops, but for videos, the website is a very good investment. They have music that sounds very professional, and once you download the music, you get to keep it forever. The website is very useful for making videos for your church, and I have yet to find another site that has as good music for videos as AudioBlocks. There do exist some free sites for music, but it is hard to find free music that can be used commercially, especially that is good quality.

Using Windows Movie Maker is simple, and once you have added your video clips in the order you want, you can add music to the video (if it's a promotional video that needs music). There are several options for adding text to the video. If a video clip is too long, you can cut the video clip where you want it cut and delete the part that you don't need. You can put your own video that you filmed in the program and use it in your video. Most phones that have cameras also have a video camera now, so it's simple to use the USB part of your phone's charger to stick into the computer and upload your video files to the computer.

One way to use video in your ministry, other than promotional videos, is to create a sermonette (a short sermon on a topic of your choice). Once you or someone else films it, you can upload it into the Windows Movie Maker program, save it as a video file, and upload it to social media. This can be posted to encourage your church members and other Christians during the week. It could be something separate from the topic of your sermon or something completely different. You can also put your church's logo in the video at the beginning, along with a short music clip that you find (as long as you have a legal copy of the music and keep within the copyright laws).

For posting videos, you can post to YouTube and/or to Vimeo, among other video websites (YouTube is the most popular, but I like Vimeo's option that allows other people to download the video onto their own computer). You can get a video link to share from YouTube or Vimeo once the video is posted there, or you can post the video directly to Facebook.

Chapter 8: Online Directories

A benefit of your church being a legal organization (which it should be, by the way) is that it is almost for sure included in the Yellow Pages. However, what not many people may know is that it is also possible to claim yourself as the "owner" or person responsible for your church on the Yellow Pages online. This will allow you to, for free, give people access to more information about your church (including updating the link to your church's website).

If your church's association has a website, they may list churches on the website. If so, make sure you mention to the administrator of the website, or the director of the association, what your church's website is. This is another free way to make sure people have updated access to your church's information.

ChurchFinder.com claims to be the best online platform for finding a church, so if this is true, it would be a good idea to see if your church is already listed on the site. If it isn't listed there, then you could add your church to their directory. If it is already there, you can claim the profile and make changes as necessary to ensure that people can get the information about your church that they need to get.

Yelp.com is a place where people review businesses. It's also a place where people find businesses. They have a section on the site for churches so it would be a great place to see if there is a listing for your church. If there is, you can claim the profile and edit it, as mentioned for the other directories.

Foursquare.com is also a free way to start a listing for your church. People can find your church this way. Basically, it's important to use a lot of the free sites to promote your church more. However, you should keep track somewhere of which sites you list your church so that, if something major changes in your church (website, service times, etc.), you have an easy time updating the directories and the websites' info. If the site has reviews or a comments section, it's also a good idea to check every now and then to see if a new review or new comment has been posted in order to decide if you need to respond to it or not.

With church directories, the most important thing is to be sure to use a wide range of directories to list your church. Most are free, so it's essentially free advertising since people do search for churches through the internet. You can even include a section on your "Welcome Guest" form that you may have first-time visitors fill out, asking how they found out about your church. Be sure to include a blank line so they can fill in how they found out if it isn't listed. Honestly, social media and the internet aren't going to probably be the main way people find out about your church, but it is still an important way to promote your church.

Part 3: Technology as a Spiritual Tool

Chapter 9: Note from the Pastor (Blogs)

Chapter 10: Online Sermon Notes

Chapter 11: Recording Your Sermons

Chapter 12: Church Online Newsletters

Chapter 13: Networking with Pastors

Chapter 9: Note from the Pastor (Blogs)

As a pastor, certainly you have more to say to your congregation than just the message you bring every Sunday morning and evening and Wednesday night. If so, you may want to consider starting a blog. In fact, your blog can reach many people who are not part of your congregation. While you can make a blog password-protected, where only certain people can read it, you can also make your blog public. If people share the blog on social media, then other people can easily find what you have written on your blog. The word blog is a combination of the two words "web" and "log," or web log. It was shortened to the word "blog."

Www.blogspot.com and www.wordpress.com are the most popular blogging sites on the internet, and they are the most used. Also, if you use Weebly for your website, you can now also make the host for your blog (there is an option in Weebly for a blog). Blogs are generally free, but if you want your own domain name for your blog, you'll have to pay a certain amount per year (depending on your domain name extension).

You could do a series of blogs based on a certain topic or write on different things different days. These posts could be like a written sermon, or they could be your own notes and style. Make sure to put a link to the blog from your church's website, especially from your personal bio on the website.

Another thing you can do to personalize the blog is to add a recorded (audio) or even videoed version of the blog. Some pastors do this, and it makes you more relatable and approachable, especially if your blog is viewed by people outside of your church and outside of your community. Plus, written communication does not convey everything and can be confusing since the intonation of the words is not easily discerned; thus, written communication can cause people to misunderstand if something is funny or unkind.

Once you have posted a lot of blog posts (or already have things that you want to put together), you could consider putting the Godly wisdom that you have obtained into a book. Self-publishing is a fairly easy endeavor (and can basically be free if you find the right companies). You don't have to start blogging to write a book, but I have heard some people use their blogs as a starting point for a book.

If you want to put your BlogSpot blog on your Weebly website, then you can use this link: http://blogname.blogspot.com/feeds/posts/default?alt=rss

Where it says "blogname," replace it with your blog's name (what goes after http:// and before .blogspot.com). For Weebly, drag the Feed Reader button from under the More section of the left column. Drag the button on the page where you want to put your blog feed and then replace their URL with the one that you just created by replacing "blogname" with your blog's name. An example with one of my blogs I have, I would now have the following link: http://jeremygwoods.blogspot.com/feeds/posts/default?alt=rss

Chapter 10: Online Sermon Notes

YouVersion has a way to set up your service notes online so that other people can follow along together at the same time. You can sign up at www.bible.com/events (they suggest that you set up a separate account for your church if you have a personal account with them). If you need to learn more about the features, you can visit https://www.bible.com/features/events.

There are other ways you can do this, including having a staff member post live on Facebook main notes from the sermon. You could also post an outline the night before using Microsoft Word and convert it to a PDF file (especially creating a partially filled in outline, where people have to come to the service to get the rest of the missing words). Also, you could post something right after the service with the outline.

Alternatively, you can time a Facebook post on a page so that the post is created at a specific time that you decide so it could appear right at, for instance, 10 a.m., just in time for the morning service. If people were to follow along on their phone, they could see the outline in front of them. This should not replace having a projected outline if you have a projector for your church and someone to run the projector.

Chapter 11: Recording Your Sermons

There are several routes you can go to make your sermons available online for people to access (even people who do not attend your church). You can choose to have audio recordings available or even have video recordings available.

A way that I have recorded some of my sermons is simply putting my phone on the pulpit next to my sermon notes/Bible and using the recording function. Most phones have a recorder tool, so it should be simple to do for most pastors. Obviously, it is not the most visually attractive thing to do by spending a few seconds to get the recorder running, but it does get the sermon recorded easily. Putting it online is easy, just by sending it to your email address. If you don't have a smartphone, then you should be able to connect your phone to your computer by using the USB stick that is probably on your phone's charger. You can then transfer the file to your computer and put the sermon online, on your church's website.

There is a free resource available to make your

church services online through video recordings: www.churchonlineplatform.com. Even their support is free, and it allows churches to host a live streaming of their services. It is amazing that there are free ways to do this, but we live in a world that is increasingly more technological, and this is now an advantage for churches, especially small churches. Another option is www.streamspot.com, which provides streaming services starting at $79 per month. They have a 30-day trial, and support is available at any subscription level, including to help you set up the streaming.

You can get the sermons videoed if you or someone in the church already has a video camera (or you can buy a decent one for $200-300 plus a tripod stand for the video camera to be stable while filming). If your church has a loft in the sanctuary, someone can film from there (that's the best place to film). If not, someone can film from the back or from one of the aisles. The videos can be put directly onto YouTube. Facebook Live also allows something to be recorded from a phone and put automatically on Facebook.

Chapter 12: Church Online Newsletters

Most churches have a weekly Sunday bulletin. However, there is probably not enough room in a Sunday bulletin to communicate what you need to communicate to your church members. Quite a few churches now use electronic newsletters to send out either once a week or once a month to people in the church (or non-church members) who sign up for the newsletter. A way to get subscribers is to put the sign-up form on the church website and to mention in church how to sign up for the newsletter (or put a sign-up sheet in the vestibule or church lobby, asking for first and last names and email addresses, and manually putting the information in yourself).

A good website for newsletters is MailChimp. They have great templates you can use; plus, they are free if you don't have more than 999 subscribers (though you may choose to have a paid plan in order to get certain statistics about the newsletters that you send out). Personally, my wife and I use MailChimp for our newsletters, and we find it very useful to use. You can put your logo at the top of the newsletter, as well as use a few graphics throughout the newsletter (not too many, so that the newsletter is not too large of a file).

Just like Weebly, MailChimp is a drag-and-drop website, which means that the things you need (text boxes, etc.) can be dragged where you need them to go. This makes it easy to use for your church. They also have an easy step-by-step process that walks the user through the process of creating a newsletter. Many organizations use MailChimp, and I highly recommend using their services for your church newsletter.

Chapter 13: Networking with Pastors

The birth of the internet has created new ways for people to connect with others in a new way. One of the best ways for pastors to connect online is through Social Media sites such as LinkedIn. LinkedIn is a free (but also offers a paid account) resource for people, particularly in the business field. However, there are groups that you can join that are for pastors around the United States and around the world to network, share ideas, and brainstorm together to become more effective ministers of the Gospel.

Facebook also has groups for pastors to join and network together. "As iron sharpens iron, so a man sharpens the countenance of his friend" (Proverbs 27:17). Fellowship is important, especially for pastors. Pastors in other regions of the United States or in other parts of the world may have different ideas on how to reach your community that you had never thought about before, and you may also be able to be a blessing to others around the world.

Part 4: Final Thoughts

Chapter 14: Don't Want to Do It Yourself?

Chapter 15: Your Church Technology Plan

Chapter 16: Dangers of Technology

Chapter 14: Don't Want to Do It Yourself?

There are several ways to get the advice from this book accomplished without having to do the methods yourself. You can hire a full-time or part-time staff member to be over Church Communications (or Church Technology), assign this task to another staff member who would be willing to put time and effort into this (plus, you could also hand the staff member this book to help him or her in getting things accomplished), or hire a company to do it for you (an example of this comes later in the chapter).

Another way you could get this done is to hire an intern in your church, someone either in college or fresh out of college. Internships can be paid or unpaid, and it is a great way to get the student/young adult job experience while your church gets help in technology and communications. This is an excellent way, also, to get more young people involved through participation in your church.

Hiring a company to do it for you can be expensive. However, one company that I have seen to provide these services is VistaPrint. They will help you start a Facebook page for $10 per month, and they offer great tools to provide easy ways to keep updating your Facebook page.

Chapter 15: Your Church Technology Plan

Do you want to implement this book effectively? If so, then you will need a plan. I am giving you a template to use for your church. You don't have to use this template, but you should start to use technology for your church, using this book as a guide. You will find the download at www.jeremyandmagdawoods.com/usingtechnologybonus.

Also included in this book is a Church Technology Plan template and a filled-out sample version of the template. Based on the Church Technology Plan, you can create a calendar based on the Example Technology Calendar.

I suggest that you download the plan, print it out, and fill it out. Be sure to keep the plan in mind as you go throughout the following months and spend a little time setting up the website and social media accounts. At the back of the book, you will find appendixes telling you how to start different social media accounts.

Church Technology Plan

Questions to be considered by pastors and church leaders for technology implementation

Name _____ Church Name _____ Date _____

Will we create a logo for our church? ☐Yes ☐No

Who will we use to create a church website? _____
Do we want to pay $10-$15 per year for a website URL? ☐Yes ☐No

Which social media platforms do we want to use as a church?
☐ Facebook   Page Name _____ Group Name _____
☐ Twitter   Twitter account name @_____
☐ Instagram   Account name _____
☐ Pinterest   Pinterest username _____
For Facebook, will we have a Facebook page (public)? ☐Yes ☐No
        Facebook group (closed/private) for members? ☐Yes ☐No

Will we create promotional videos for our church? ☐Yes ☐No
Will we create preview videos for the Sunday sermon? ☐Yes ☐No

Will we put church info on online directories? ☐Yes ☐No
Will the pastor keep up a blog? ☐Yes ☐No
        If so, which site will the blog be on? _____

Will we update sermon notes during the sermon? ☐Yes ☐No
        If so, how? _____
Will we record our sermons? ☐Yes ☐No
Will we videotape our sermons? ☐Yes ☐No

Will we use an electronic newsletter to send out? ☐Yes ☐No
        If yes, what website will we use? _____

Will the pastor network with other pastors online? ☐Yes ☐No
If so, where? ☐Facebook ☐LinkedIn ☐Twitter ☐Other _____

Who will do technology/multimedia? Any combination of these:
☐Pastor ☐Church Leader ☐Church Member ☐Intern ☐Volunteer
☐Hire a company ☐Create new tech staff member position in church
☐Other _____

What should be the church technology budget? _____

© Jeremy G. Woods 2017, from Using Technology for Your Church: A Guide for Pastors and Church Leaders

This technology plan can be downloaded at:

www.jeremyandmagdawoods.com/usingtechnologybonus.

Church Technology Plan

Questions to be considered by pastors and church leaders for technology implementation

Name _Jeremy G. Woods_ Church Name _Test Plan_   Date _March 17 2017_

Will we create a logo for our church? ☑Yes ☐No

Who will we use to create a church website? _Weebly_
Do we want to pay $10-$15 per year for a website URL? ☑Yes ☐No

Which social media platforms do we want to use as a church?
☑ Facebook   Page Name _Test Page_   Group Name _Test Group_
☑ Twitter   Twitter account name @ _TestAccount_
☑ Instagram   Account name _TestAccount_
☑ Pinterest   Pinterest username _TestAccount_
For Facebook, will we have a Facebook page (public)? ☑Yes ☐No
      Facebook group (closed/private) for members? ☑Yes ☐No

Will we create promotional videos for our church? ☑Yes ☐No
Will we create preview videos for the Sunday sermon? ☑Yes ☐No

Will we put church info on online directories? ☑Yes ☐No
Will the pastor keep up a blog? ☑Yes ☐No
      If so, which site will the blog be on? _test.blogspot.com_

Will we update sermon notes during the sermon? ☑Yes ☐No
      If so, how? _YouVersion Event_
Will we record our sermons? ☐Yes ☑No
Will we videotape our sermons? ☑Yes ☐No

Will we use an electronic newsletter to send out? ☑Yes ☐No
      If yes, what website will we use? _MailChimp_

Will the pastor network with other pastors online? ☑Yes ☐No
If so, where? ☑Facebook ☑LinkedIn ☐Twitter ☐Other _____

Who will do technology/multimedia? Any combination of these:
☑Pastor ☑Church Leader ☐Church Member ☐Intern ☑Volunteer
☐Hire a company ☐Create new tech staff member position in church
☐Other _____

What should be the church technology budget? _$300 per month_

© Jeremy G. Woods 2017, from Using Technology for Your Church: A Guide for Pastors and Church Leaders

This is an example of a filled-out Church Technology Plan template. Once again, the template can be downloaded for free here at this website:

www.jeremyandmagdawoods.com/usingtechnologybonus.

Example Technology Calendar - MMYY						
Monday	Tuesday	Wednesday	Thursday	Friday	Saturday	Sunday
1 Put up Sunday sermon	2 Create graphic Put it up on social media	3 Record a mid-week sermonette and put it on social media	4 Throw-back Thursday older photo	5	6 Post preview video for sermon	7 Record sermon
8 Put up Sunday sermon	9 Create graphic Put it up on social media	10 Record a mid-week sermonette and put it on social media	11 Throw-back Thursday – older photo	12	13 Post preview video for sermon	14 Record sermon
15 Put up Sunday sermon	16 Create graphic Put it up on social media	17 Record a mid-week sermonette and put it on social media	18 Throw-back Thursday – older photo	19	20 Post preview video for sermon	21 Record sermon
22 Put up Sunday sermon	23 Create graphic Put it up on social media	24 Record a mid-week sermonette and put it on social media	25 Throw-back Thursday – older photo	26	27 Post preview video for sermon	28 Record sermon
29 Put up Sunday sermon	30 Create graphic Put it up on social media	31 Record a mid-week sermonette and put it on social media				

This is a sample filled-out calendar (you can use a regular calendar).

Chapter 16: Dangers of Technology

This book would not be complete if I did not tell the other side of getting involved with technology. One important thing to mention is that whatever is put on the internet remains where someone can see it. Even things that are deleted are still somewhere in Cyberspace, accessible for someone who knows how to access them.

Also, putting information publicly on the internet about people is not wise, especially without their permission.

Once you get involved with the internet, especially Social Media, it is very hard to stop using it unless you have self-control. There's always one more thing that you can do on Facebook, always one more quick thing you can do to promote your church, always one more quick way to contact someone. Also, it is fun to get to see updates from people. If you're not careful, you could spend all day on Facebook and not get the things done that you need to get done. Facebook (and social media) are great tools, but if they become too personal, they can become very addictive.

Sometimes, the more you get involved with technology, the more you must spend to resolve problems, get updates, or make the technology work. You don't usually have to spend the money for updates; it's just usually a temptation to keep spending money to improve the technology you already own. Make sure to keep within your church's budget or else use your own money for things that you want for the church.

Another big thing is that just about everything is on the internet, and a major ministry killer is pornography. There are site blockers on the internet that will make the internet safer for you as a pastor or church leader. I would highly suggest putting something like this on your browser, especially if you are prone to be tempted.

Appendixes

Appendix 1: How to Start an Email Account

Appendix 2: How to Start a Website with Weebly

Appendix 3: How to Start a Facebook Account/Profile

Appendix 4: How to Start a Facebook Page

Appendix 5: How to Start a Facebook Group

Appendix 6: How to Start a Twitter Account

Appendix 7: How to Start an Instagram Account

Appendix 8: How to Start a Pinterest Account

Appendix 1: How to Start an Email Account

There are many email providers, but I will mention how to start a Gmail account in this book. It's probably very similar for other email account providers.

- Go to www.google.com
- On the top-right corner, click Gmail
- Click "Create an account" at the top right corner
- Type in your First and Last names, choose your username (which will be part of your email address) and password (and enter the password a second time to confirm it), and put in your birthday and gender
- They want your mobile (cell) phone so that they can send you a text confirmation to your phone, so put your mobile phone number there
- If you're reading this, I assume that you haven't had an email address before, so you should be able to leave the text box blank where they ask you for your current email address

- There is a check box under the request for your current email address that sets Google as your default homepage; unclick the box, unless you want Google to pop up every time you open your browser (personally, I like that option, but not everybody does)
- Your location should already be put in the next box, but if not, go ahead and change it; then hit the "Next Step" button
- Read and accept the Privacy and Terms
- You should see a welcome screen; press "Continue to Gmail" and start using your email account; use the username as what you put before @gmail.com (e.g. pastor@gmail.com)
- Be sure to put a link to the email address on the church's website when you make the website

Appendix 2: How to Start a Website with Weebly

There are many ways you can make a website, but since I can't mention all of them, I will mention the way that I use (you can do a simple search on the internet to find many ways to make a website).

- Go to www.weebly.com
- Click "Sign Up" at the top-right corner of the page
- You can use Facebook or Google+ to help you sign up, or you can manually enter your name, email address, and choose a password you want to use to enter
- Press "Sign Up.
- Select a theme that you want to use for the website; there are many themes, and you can also click near the top whether you want to search through "Online Store," "Business," etc.
- Once you like the theme, click it and hit "Start Boarding"
- Choose if you will have a domain name

(probably around $10-$15 per year) — e.g. www.yoursitenamehere.com - or have your site on Weebly (where it would look something like this website address: www.yoursitenamehere.weebly.com). In my opinion, it's easier to have the domain name (it's easier for people to remember how to get to the website)
- To get a domain name, you'll need to get one from GoDaddy.com (and they have customer support that can help you get a website and get it set up on Weebly.com)
- To use the one hosted on Weebly.com, select your name (as a subdomain of Weebly) and hit the "Continue" button
- Look around Weebly and drag the buttons to the left to the page to add text boxes, videos, photos, etc. and when you're ready, hit "Publish"; you can always log in and make changes as needed
- Make sure to put something on each page

- You can edit the names of pages on the "Pages" button at the top of the page
- In the website editor, you can press the "Help" button at the top of the page to contact or call for support, and they can answer questions that you have

Appendix 3: How to Start a Facebook Account/Profile

If you don't have a Facebook profile yet, one can be created in a few minutes (and then you just keep building it up regularly, though it doesn't have to be daily).

- Go to www.facebook.com
- Enter your first and last name, cell phone number or email address, password you choose, birthday, and your gender, then hit sign up
- If you chose email address, you would need to confirm your email address by clicking the link sent to you, and if you chose phone number, then a text should be sent to your phone, and you will need to follow the instructions to get your account activated
- You will be asked to put in more information about yourself, including your profile picture, which is what photo will be beside your name when you write a post on Facebook; you can fill in as much as you want and make your profile as

private as you want through privacy settings

Appendix 4: How to Start a Facebook Page

- To start a Facebook page, you log in to your Facebook account and click the button "Pages" on the left side of the page, under the heading "Explore"
- You will see a button that says "Create Page" at the top right of the page
- You will then want to select the 2nd option, which is "Company, Organization, or Institution"
- You then want to click the "drop-down box that appears in the space where "Company, Organization, or Institution" was. You should scroll down in that box to where "Religious Organization" is and click
- Type your church's name below the drop-down box
- Read the Terms and Conditions and put a checkmark that you agree with them (if you do)
- Click "Get Started"
- Add a profile picture (graphic, photo of your

church, etc.)
- Add a cover photo for the page
- Add a short description (this can be anything you want)
- Click "Add a Button" on the right of the page
  o Click "Learn More" and then, given the two options, click "Learn More" again if you want to add your church's website to the button link
  o Click in the box labeled "Add a Website Link" and put the URL of your church's website: (e.g. https://www.yourchurchnamehere.org)
- "Like" the page on Facebook (so that others are aware of the page on your Facebook's News Feed
- Click on the button on the top of the page that looks like … Then click on "Edit the page"
- Click on "Page Category" (you can change it to reflect your denomination – just remove "Religious Organization" from the text box and type in your denomination; it's probably in the list; if not, you can choose the term "Church")

- Fill in the description
- Fill in Contact phone number, website, email address, address of your church, and hours (for hours, you can select which days you have services and list the hours) - you can press the + near the hours section to add more times that day that the church is open
- Click the link at the bottom of the page "See All Information" to get to a different page with more information that you can update.
- Choose a username for the page (there can't be any spaces) – this will become the website address for your church on Facebook (e.g. www.facebook.com/yourchurchnamehere)
- You can update the section called "Your Story" (this could be more info about the church or even the history of the church if you want)
- Click on "Promote" on your Facebook page
  o Click on "Share Page with Friends" to invite them
  o Get people to "like" the page – especially

church members (you must be friends with people on Facebook to invite them to "like" the Facebook page, but you can announce to the church members that there is a new Facebook page). Even other people in the community or other pastors or Christians may be willing to "like" the page on Facebook.

- If you click on the button at the top of your Facebook page, "Settings," then you will be able to see many, many more options to change on your Facebook page – you can even add people as administrators to change the Facebook page as well

Appendix 5: How to Start a Facebook Group

- To start a Facebook group, you log in to your Facebook account and click the button "Groups" on the left side of the page, under the heading "Explore," directly under "Pages"
- On the top right of the next page, click "Create Group"
- Give your group a name (something related to your church)
- For this, unlike for Facebook Pages, you have to invite someone to the group before you can finish creating the group.
- Choose the group privacy (Public, Private, or Closed) – You probably want the group to be private or closed so that only the church members can see the posts (your Facebook page can be the public face of your church, while the Facebook group may be where members share Bible verses, prayer requests, etc.)
- Create the group and select the group's icon

(though you can skip that section if you want)
- Once in, you can add more people, make posts, etc.
- Facebook has more information in the help section if you still need help

Appendix 6: How to Start a Twitter Account

- Go to www.twitter.com (or use the app on your phone)
- Create a new account
- Type your name (Church name), email/cell phone #, and create a password)
- Verify the email account or cell phone # when the email or text is sent to you
- Edit the account – edit the name (if you need to), create a username, edit your bio (info about the church), etc.
- Follow people/organizations on Twitter that you want to follow, including church members
- Follow this book (@churchtechbook) and the author (@jeremygwoods) if you want

Appendix 7: How to Start an Instagram Account

- Go to www.instagram.com
- You can log in through Facebook (therefore connecting the accounts) or enter the information manually
- If you choose to enter the information manually, type in your cell phone # or email (for verification), full name, and choose a username and a password to log in; hit the "Sign up" button.
- Follow the rest of the instructions once you get a verification email or text. You will need a smartphone app to post photos on Instagram, but you can view photos from the website

Appendix 8: How to Start a Pinterest Account

- Log into www.pinterest.com
- Type in your email address and create a password and hit "Continue" or sign in using your Facebook account
- Follow the instructions in the email that you receive.
- You will be able to follow people on Pinterest, particularly people from the church if they are on; also, you can make categories of your posts (e.g. Encouragement, Events, Bible Quotes, etc.)

Bibliography

Clark, Jerod. "Church Website Statistics." *Christian Reformed Church in North America*. 1 Aug. 2012. Web. 03 Mar. 2017. <http://network.crcna.org/church-web/church-website-statistics>.

Just Creative. "Branding, Identity & Logo Design Explained." *JUST™ Creative*. Just Creative, 06 Apr. 2010. Web. 13 Mar. 2017. <http://justcreative.com/2010/04/06/branding-identity-logo-design-explained/>.

Masci, David. *What Do Americans Look for in a Church, and How Do They Find One? It Depends in Part on Their Age*. Rep. Pew Research Center, 23 Aug. 2016. Web. 3 Mar. 2017.

"Multimedia." *Merriam-Webster.com*. Merriam-Webster. Web. 3 Mar. 2017.

New King James Version. Bible Gateway. Web. 22 March. 2017.

"Technology." *Merriam-Webster.com*. Merriam-Webster. Web. 3 Mar. 2017.

About the Author

Jeremy G. Woods was born in Huntsville, Alabama. He graduated from Grissom High School and from the University of North Alabama with a major in marketing and a minor in French. He has taken seminary classes (including a class on Christian preaching). He was an interim preacher at a church in Huntsville, Alabama, for several months and has preached in several churches.

He currently lives in Târgu Mureş, Romania, with his wife, Magda, who is from Romania. Jeremy and Magda were missionaries in Romania (Jeremy moved overseas and met Magda while on the mission field), and they both currently write books and run a new company, FaithVenture Media. Jeremy and Magda are expecting their first child.

Jeremy has a background in making websites as well as running several pages and groups on Facebook. The website for this book is: www.helpingchurchesgrow.org/churchtechbook. "Helping Churches Grow" is his new website/blog to help small or struggling churches grow Spiritually and in number. Jeremy and Magda have co-founded and co-own a new company called FaithVenture Media, a company that publishes Christian books, creates promo videos and websites for churches, ministries, and companies, and produces Christian music in Romanian, French, and English.

Made in the USA
Columbia, SC
15 July 2021